S. Bienenstok

Robert Churchill

S. Bienenstok

Robert Churchill

ISBN/EAN: 9783743326927

Manufactured in Europe, USA, Canada, Australia, Japa

Cover: Foto ©ninafisch / pixelio.de

Manufactured and distributed by brebook publishing software
(www.brebook.com)

S. Bienenstok

Robert Churchill

ROBERT CHURCHILL

IN

FIVE ACTS.

CHARACTERS.

MRS. CHURCHILL, ... A Widow.

REGINALD, ... Her Son.

ROBERT, ... Her Step-son.

BEATRICE, ... Her Daughter.

LADY DORA PERCIVAL.

LORD AUGUSTUS MANDEVILLE.

PRENTISS CARRINGTON, ... His Nephew

SIR GLADWOLD.

SERVANT.

SCENE : *England, near London.*

ROBERT CHURCHILL.

ACT I.

SCENE.—*Residence of the Churchills. A finely furnished apartment. Open* C. *doors. Doors* R. *and* L. *and a window* L. *upper entrance. Sofa left hand under window.*

[*Enter* REGINALD, C.]

REG. I have not closed my eyes this night. The fear of approaching evil weighs upon my spirit and destroys my rest. Behind transgression's luring front remorse steals like a thief. Oh, I wish I had no conscience, for 'tis a careless monitor at best that gives alarm when the deed has slipped and help comes in too late. I owe Wrexford 5000*l.*—5000*l.*! How tremendous that amount now seems, how little in spending it. He led me on, placed a ready purse at my disposal ; I betted, I raced, I gambled. I would pretend the gentleman and so betrayed the fool. My follies bore fine fruit. I fell a ready victim to a villain's wiles, and he plucked me bare. That money I must have or else publish my own disgrace in the ruin of my family. But how ?

[*Enter* MRS. CHURCHILL *and* BEATRICE, L. *door.*]

MRS. C. Are you here yet, Reginald, and in this costume ? What is the matter with you lately ; you are getting as neglectful of yourself as an old man. There is something troubling you.

REG. (R.) Nothing of the kind, mother—pure imagination, I assure you.

BEAT. (L.) Pure imagination, is it ? Is that what keeps you pacing your room night after night, so I can't sleep ? I don't believe a word of it. You must be nursing some dreadful secret. Or, tell me, dear, are you in love ? I heard that is one of the symptoms.

REG. You have heard too much, or may be you speak from experience.

BEAT. There you are, always as disagreeable as can be—a person can't get a sensible word out of you.

MRS. C. Somehow your brother's coming appears to me like an evil omen to this house.

BEAT. Mother, why?

MRS. C. I don't know. Somehow I never could bring myself to love the shy and gloomy child your father presented to me the day he brought me to his home. Perhaps it was because your father was partial to his eldest born that I disliked the boy.

BEAT. You did not drive him from you, mother?

MRS. C. Your father died leaving an encumbered estate. All the money I had was my own, and though I considered the support of his child a burden to me, I conscientiously provided for his education. When Robert returned from college he saw how unwelcome he was at my house and table; and I really do not remember how it came about that he accepted an offer to go to America, and left us with but a cold farewell. I have since heard that he has made a fortune there. Now he comes back to visit us, bringing with him a young girl whom he has adopted—the daughter of an actor.

BEAT. How touchingly Robert writes of her. I am so anxious to know this orphan, to extend to the poor girl the hand of devoted friendship.

MRS. C. We shall receive her on his account. But he will be disappointed if he imagines that we shall parade this obscure offspring of the stage as our equal before the world.

BEAT. But, mother, we cannot humiliate Robert's ward. Remember we have accepted frequent favors from him.

MRS. C. He has not half repaid the debt he owes to me. Besides is it not sufficiently humiliating to have it broached about that one of our family is earning his living in trade and common barter.

REG. Well, mother, he has money, and that is in itself a sufficient excuse for the means of making it, even in this country. As for this ward of his, I shall not forget to conduct myself toward her as a gentleman—if she be a lady ; if not, she sinks below our level, and propping will do no good.   At any rate Robert has given us frequent indications of his good-will, and for that reason alone he should be well received.

MRS. C. Be sure 1 shall not make a prodigal of him. I have some distinctly unpleasant recollections about him.   You will learn to know him too.

BEAT. I don't remember anything of Robert ; still I can respect him who, disclaiming the vain advantages of birth, fights his way upward without a helping hand. To me he seems like a hero.

MRS. C. Well, well ; we shall see how he conducts himself.   In the meantime I go to give some orders for the rooms our guests shall occupy.   I'll need you, Beatrice.

[*Crosses* L. *and exeunt* MRS. CHURCHILL *and* BEATRICE, L. *door.*]

REG. (C.) Come, come, shake off this cowardly ap-prehension.   What a sloth I am to stagger so under the evil I have laid upon myself. I have bartered comfort for doubtful luxuries, spurned ease for excitement.   I surrendered myself with zest to degrading pleasures until virtue became shabby to my eyes and I grew to be ashamed of her.   I have one resort.   Robert is rich, and he must help me out.

[*Enter* SERVANT, C. *door* L.]

SERV. Mr. Prentiss Carrington !
REG. Show him in.   [*Exit* SERVANT.

[*Enter* CARRINGTON, C. *door.*]

CAR. (L.) Hallo, Bob, old boy, where have you been all week ? How did you get over Lady Flora's party, aye ? I got dreadfully tipsy that night, fell asleep just about morning on a sofa in one of the ante-rooms ; woke up to rush down in time to miss the morning drill, and get one of those famous knock down lectures from our old grizzly bear of a captain, that falls on one's ears like the hoarse dolings of a funeral bell.

REG. (R.) There you go like a steam-engine.   To hear you talk one would think that you were ignorant of my troubles or that you had no heart.

' CAR. Sure enough, I had forgotten all about it. Do you know really that I sometimes believe I have no heart ? That is, when you consider the heart as an organ that should throb in unison with other similar affairs, or that should sympathize with the joys and sufferings of others. Bobby, it isn't there. I am, if not physically speaking, an absolute heartless man. Can you consider yourself hurt because I do not feel for you in your affliction, when I could learn of the serious illness of an aged maiden aunt, one of the numerous nearest relatives I have on earth, without the least flutter of excitement—yea, even learn of her melancholy demise without any other feeling than that of disgust at the contemptible legacy she had left me ? Require anything of me, but do not—I pray you, do not ask me to feel for you.

REG. I have no need of anything now but money.

CAR. Money ? That is something I haven't got. You have already helped yourself so liberally from my income that I shall have to live on regimental rations for six months to come.

REG. Why didn't you tell me so ? I thought you were well off.

CAR. That depends upon how you take it. Just now I am considerably off. I have departed from the trodden path of rectitude in contracting certain debts which my ancient and deplorable—I mean adorable uncle—Lord Augustus Mandeville was called upon to pay. This he has done, but in punishment stopped my monthly allowance and banished me from his august presence until I have given sufficient proof of having improved my hitherto graceless career. This puts me in a fix, and prevents my soliciting him to help you out of this scrape.

REG. I shall endeavor to get the assistance of my stepbrother Robert, whom we expect here from America today. I hear that he has lots of money. Our equipage waits for him at the station now. You must excuse me until I get myself a little trimmed up for the occasion. Make yourself at home. Mother and Beatrice will be in soon.

CAR. Go on, I can take care of myself. (*Exit* REG. R. *door.*) How selfish misery makes a man ! He

nurses his own affliction and little heeds the deeper grief
that here abides.

> Divine emotion, essential part of joy,
> Heart's inspiration and the soul's decoy,
> Sweet breath of heaven, Love, 'tis thee I feel.

Yes ! love, 'tis thee I feel ! How does it go on ?

> Firmly and securely deep within my heart,
> There you have entered never to depart.

I have been trying to soften my soul with poetry, but no
use ; my feelings are too coarse for that ; my face must
show it plainly. (*Goes* R.) Even this looking-glass reflects it. Tell me, thou silent revealer of our physical
imperfections, what claim have I, an impecunious sub-
officer in the queen's service, to the regard of this young
lady, a non-commissioned spirit of grace, an angel by
virtue's patent and beauty's signature ? Let me see.
Handsome I am certainly not, and with my face alone as
pleader my chances would be rather slim—about as slim
as my figure. If I could only discover in myself a single
redeeming trait that I could gloss over and embellish so
as to hang out for a sign. Would it do to tell her ? I
admit I am not good-looking, neither am I very grace-
ful, neither am I very sensible, neither have I ever done
a single thing to recommend me to anybody's favor ; yet
on the other hand, and to counterbalance all these defects, I am as poor as a church mouse, and summing it
all up—a most presumptuous youth.

[*Enter* BEATRICE, L. *door.*]

BEAT. (L.) Mr. Carrington ! I was not aware that
you were making your toilet here, but can't I assist you
to better accommodations ?   .

CAR. (R.) I ? Me ? Oh, no ! I make my toilet
here ? On the contrary—I was not making my toilet
here.

BEAT. Oh, I see, you were simply admiring yourself
in the glass. Ah ! how I envy you for having as much
beauty to admire !

CAR. Oh, yes ! I must admit, I have beauty to
admire.

BEAT. Oh, a great deal.

CAR. Certainly a great deal.

' BEAT. (*Indignantly.*) Where?

CAR. Before me of course—how else could I mean it?

BEAT. That was nicely turned. I appreciate the compliment. But people wouldn't believe you.

CAR. Wouldn't they? Now I'd like that—

BEAT. What would you like?

CAR. That to all the world except myself you would appear different than you are. I could bless the man that called you ugly.

BEAT. Well upon my word, you have a pronounced talent for saying disagreeable things.

CAR. So I have, Miss Churchill—at least when in your presence. Just when I try the hardest to make myself pleasant I am sure to make a failure of it.

BEAT. Then it might be a good idea not to try, or with this result for a guide, suppose you try the other way—try not to please me; you would perhaps then succeed in making yourself somewhat bearable.

CAR. Miss Churchill, can you compass the ambition of him who would grasp the unattainable, analyze the yearnings of earth-bound man to things celestial and divine? Can you imagine the pain the stricken heart must feel when it realizes that the object of its devotion is beyond its reach—perhaps beyond its meed? Can you—oh, can you—imagine the desperation—

[*Enter* MRS. CHURCHILL, L. *door and crosses to* C.]

MRS. C. I am pleased to see you, Mr. Carrington.

CAR. Oh, how do you do, Mrs. Churchill?

MRS. C. Excuse the interruption, but I thought I heard the rumble of wheels.

[BEATRICE *runs to window.*

BEAT. Oh look, mamma; there he is alighting from the carriage. There are two ladies with him, maid and mistress it must be; for one jumps out herself, and he assists the other—oh, so tenderly. She seems shy to advance, and laughingly he pushes her before him. They are coming up the steps, and now they are in the house. (*To* SERVANT *who appears at the door.*) Oh, don't stand there like a dummy—don't you see you are to show them in at once ?　　　　　　　　　　　*[Exit* SERVANT.

CAR. This sun puts my faint light into eclipse. I shall very discreetly retire.　　　　　　*[Exit* C. *door.*

[BEATRICE *rushes to door, then checks herself.*

[*Enter* ROBERT *and* MARGARET, C. *door* L.]

ROB. (C.) Come on. No vain attraction draws you on to me. I know not who you are, yet something tells me I have the right to clasp you in my arms. (*Embraces* BEATRICE. *Then goes to his mother,* L. *of* C., *while* BEATRICE *salutes* MARGARET.). But, mother, the word of welcome first belongs to you. We parted coldly, yet time, that mellows everything, must soften feelings too. Experiences oft will reverence the ties that youth ignores. Now teach me, mother, how to be a son—to love my father in my father's wife.

MRS. C. I give you welcome, Robert, with all my heart. I never gave you cause for your estrangement, and confiding now in your intent, most willingly forget the past. This is your sister Beatrice.

ROB. This is the baby I have so often fondled in my arms, shot out in blossoms like a flower o'ernight ! I don't forget you, Margaret. Don't be so shy ; this is your future home. My ward, mother ; and Beatrice, your sister that is to be. (*Passes her between the two ladies and walks* R. *of* C.)

BEAT. I have read of you so much in Robert's letters that I feel as if we were already old acquaintances, and though I have not even heard your voice, my heart leans toward you, and so, unasked, I give you tender of my love. Won't you kiss me, Margaret ?

MAR. I cannot tell you what I wish to say.

BEAT. Don't say it then. I hunger for a sister such as you, and with my whims I yet may tire a nature sweet as yours.

ROB. I have not had occasion, perhaps the inclination, to frequent society, and for that reason Margaret's life has been very retired. You will, won't you, make up for my neglect, as I wish Margaret to see our English world and taste its pleasures to their full extent.

Mrs. C. I shall endeavor to do my duty toward your ward, but make no promise that I cannot answer for.

Mar. I have no claim upon you, Mrs. Churchill, and will do my best not to tax your kindness too heavily.

Beat. There, there, sit down. (*Seats her on sofa.*) You must be very tired and hungry too, dear—dear, how thoughtless of me ; we have a repast prepared for your arrival. I'll run in to see if it is served. I'll not be long.   [*Exit* l. *door*.

Rob. I've quite forgotten Reginald. Where is he ?

Mrs. C. (l. *of* c.) He is dressing, and will be down in a moment.

Rob. It hardly seems like fifteen years since I have left this house. Reginald must be quite a young man ?

Mrs. C. You were but a lad yourself when you left home. What a change fifteen years can make ! You must have had great troubles, for you look above your age, Robert. If I mistake not, you are within a month of thirty-six.

Rob. Thirty-six ! so old ; and only thirty-six. I've been a gambler, mother. I've staked my years for fortune and won some gold and more gray hairs. See, mother, the livery of decay already streaks these temples.

[*Enter* Servant, c.]

Ser. There's a individual down-stairs as says he has a message for Mr. Churchill.

Mrs. C. Why did you not take it from him and bring it in ?

Ser. I did ask him for it, ma'am, but he says he was told to give it to Mr. Robert Churchill in person and must obey instructions.

Rob. Perhaps it is a cablegram from America. I shall see what the man wants. (*To* Servant.) Lead the way.   [*Exeunt* Robert *and* Servant.

Mrs. C. The long and tedious voyage, with its attendant sickness, is a great trial ; still such an attentive companion as Robert must have relieved many of the inconveniences of travel.

Mar. (*Rising.*) Indeed, Mrs. Churchill, you do not know how good Robert is. He seems to know my every want and wish and take delight to shame me with his own great unselfishness.

Mrs. C. This sounds nice ; so much disinterested love on one side, and such profound appreciation on the other. It is like the story of Paul and Virginia.

Mar. Do you find our attachment so singular ?

Mrs. C. Oh no, not at all—only worldly minded people are likely to sneer at it ; and if you are an example, I might conclude that the American are much less sophisticated than our average English ladies.

Mar. Why should the world deride the trust a noble man inspires in woman's heart ?

Mrs. C. You appear to know little of the world as yet. We must be very careful. Society is naturally suspicious, and actions that seem proper to ourselves may give rise to unpleasant reports.

Mar. Should we repress our better natures because there are some who seek an evil motive in the purest and most generous deed ?

Mrs. C. You misunderstand. I shall explain my meaning better some other time. Here comes Reginald.

[*Enter* Reginald, R. *door.*]

Reg. Where is Robert ? This must be his ward.

Mrs. C. (c.) Miss Margaret Hastings, my son, Mr. Reginald Churchill.

Reg. (R. *Aside*). By Jove ! but she's a beauty—no wonder Robert thinks so much of her. (*Loud.*) You must call me Reginald, for I intend to take advantage of our coming intimacy and call you Margaret at once.

(Mrs. C. *coughs as if to interrupt him, and gives him a reproving look, which* Margaret *notices.*)

[*Enter* Beatrice, L. *door.*]

Beat. Dinner is waiting. Come, Margaret ; we have kept you fasting too long already. Where has Robert gone ?

[*Enter* Robert, C. *bearing a letter.*]

Reg. (*Advancing to him,* C.) Robert, my brother, I am glad to see you home again.

Rob. (C. *Disregarding* Reginald's *proffered hand, tenders him letter coldly.*) Read !

MAR. (L. C.)   What makes you look so pale, Robert ?
Your hand feels cold as ice.

ROB. (*Whispering to* REGINALD.)   To what associa-
tions have you sunk ?   How came you to contract such
debts ?

REG. (*Aside.*)   'Tis my Mephisto's hand again.   He
wants the money due him, or threatens to bring suit and
so disgrace me.

MRS. C. (R.)   Well, let us dine.   Are you coming
in ?   Why, what is the matter ?   Tell me, Reginald,
what does this mean ?

REG.   What does it mean ?   How should I know ?

MRS. C.   There is some evil that impends that both
your faces show.

ROB.   Don't be too hasty.

MRS. C.   Then let me see this letter ; if it concerns
you, Reginald, it must concern me too.

REG.   It is not for me.

MRS. C.   For whom, then ?

REG.   For whom is it ?   It is addressed to you,
brother. (*Entreatingly.*)   Brother, it belongs to you.

ROB.   To me ? (*Low.*)   So may it be (*loud*) : it is for
me.   Come, you must go with me to London—straight.

BEAT.   What ! without the dinner ?   Poor Margaret,
you have a strange reception.

END OF ACT I.

ACT II.

SCENE.—*Ball at the Percival mansion.   An elegant
apartment with* C. *doors and set door* L. 2 E.   *Chairs,
sofa, etc.*

[*Enter* MRS. CHURCHILL *and* LADY DORA PERCIVAL,
L. U. E.]

DORA. (L.)   It is getting late ; the guests are all
assembled, and Robert is not here yet.   I wonder what
can be keeping him so long.

Mrs. C. (r.) He promised to return at eight. There is some important business that takes him frequently to London, though what it is I never can imagine.

Dora. Then we must go on without him. Aunty, why did you bring that girl with you ? I thought I showed her plainly by my looks that I do not care for her society.

Mrs. C. You mean Margaret Hastings ? I could not slight her : that would offend Robert.

Dora. He must think a great deal of her.

Mrs. C. Very much, it seems !

Dora. She is of the kind that can ingratiate themselves with such dupes as he.

Mrs. C. She has not impressed you favorably.

Dora. She cannot deceive me with those soft eyes which shrink from every gaze. .

Mrs. C. Her influence with Robert is very strong.

Dora. Well, I can use the same arts she does, and once I feel myself the mistress there, I'll show her what she least expects. (*Music sounds.*) Listen ! the music is striking up. Let us go in. [*Exit* l. u. e.

[*Enter* Robert, r. u. e.]

Rob. This Thomas Wrexford is a bold, shrewd fellow. I could do nothing with him. However, I left the whole matter to my agent, who will checkmate the scoundrel's designs for the present, and possibly induce him to sign off his claim on payment of part of the amount. (*Looks* l. u. e. *while putting on his gloves.*) The hall is brilliantly lit up. I wonder if I shall feel myself at ease in such a dazzling crowd. Already the music seems to soften my reflection, and a strange weird feeling steals over me. How sweet the low impressive strain upon our fervent fancies rings, what grand effects does it attain, attuned to harmony within. It blossoms from the heart into the world, thoughts sink in dreams and spring outstrips its season. We see it beaming in the happy smile, glistening in affection's tears, and feel its thrilling in the kiss. Thou all-inspiring melody, under thy influence faith becomes holier still, and love grows more divine.

[*Enter* REGINALD, L. U. E., *who walks slowly up behind him.*]

REG. (L.) Robert !

ROB. (*Turns impatiently.*) Well, what is it now ?

REG. What have you done in London ? You do not know my anxiety—how uneasy and wretched I feel.

ROB. This is not the place to talk about it. I must go in.   [*Exit* L. 2 F.

REG. He treats me like a criminal.   [*Exit* L. 2 E.

[*Enter* LORD MANDEVILLE *and* LADY CHURCHILL, L. U. E.]

MRS. C. (L.) You see, Lady Dora's father and Robert's were cousins. Robert was a favorite of Lord Percival, and spent most of his vacation at his uncle's house. The two children were attached to each other in spite of the difference in their ages. In fact, it was understood that they were eventually to become a pair, and this was almost a compact between the parents, and my husband's dearest wish expressed when on his dying bed.

MAN. (R.) And so this party is in honor of your son's return. Beautiful thought ! He swam the ocean to meet his love, like another Leander to his Hero. Byron doubts the story. Do you believe in ancient mythology, Mrs. Churchill ?

MRS. C. I do not believe in talking so much about it, Lord Mandeville. If I am not mistaken you have asked me that question about every time we have met.

MAN. Did I indeed ? What a remarkable coincidence that is ! We philosophers are such absent - minded people. You have heard the story about La Fontaine, the author of the Fables, setting out to visit a friend at whose funeral he had been only a few days before ?

MRS. C. I think your lordship has also kindly entertained me with that story before.

MAN. Well, then, as another illustration, have I ever in the strain of absent-mindedness alluded to the affection that I entertain for your daughter, Miss Beatrice ?

MRS. C. If I recollect aright, your lordship has alluded to it—only in moments of abstraction, of course. I beg your pardon, had we not better return to the ball-room ?

MAN. Not yet, if you please ; we are just getting

nicely to the point of our conference. It is of your daughter I wish to speak. For the first time in the course of my existence I have felt the sting of Cupid's arrow. Madam, I love your daughter so much, as much —as I hate my nephew. Madame, do you know what it is to have a designing relative ; one whose only aim in life apparently is to destroy his uncle's peace and wrestle with the rotundity of his pocket-book ?

MRS. C. It seems your lordship is again slightly wandering from the subject.

MAN. Let me explain. (*Goes* R. *with her.*)

[*Enter* CARRINGTON, L. U. E., *and remains back.*]

MRS. C. Not so loud ; some one is coming—this way.

CAR. (*Sotto voce.*) I was born under an unlucky star. I have not been able to come near Beatrice once to-night. Always some one to get ahead of me. (*Seeing* MANDEVILLE *with* MRS. C.) I wonder if the old cad is making love to Mrs. Churchill?

MAN. I admit that I want to spoil the young profligate's chances of becoming my heir ; but the love I bear your daughter is as sincere as the passion the Trajan Troilus felt for his Cressida.

MRS. C. Your lordship can become quite eloquent on occasions.

MAN. Remember 'tis love that gives me inspiration.

CAR. (*Sotto voce.*) Is it ? I shouldn't judge so if the nose is any indication.

MAN. You will assist me in gaining your daughter's hand ?

CAR. (*Sotto voce.*) What ! the daughter ? Heavens, I faint !

MRS. C. Your lordship's proposal is an honor both to my daughter and myself.

CAR. (*Sotto voce.*) And a death-blow to me.

MAN. Madam, you will make me the happiest man in all England.

CAR. (*Sotto voce.*) And me the most miserable.

[*Enter* BEATRICE *and* SIR GLADWOLD, L. U. E.]

BEAT. (*To* GLADWOLD.) I must insist upon your leaving me. I would not for the world deprive the other ladies of such an admirable partner. (*Both down* L.)

CAR. (*Sotto voce.*) With this man still. Oh, I shall be revenged ; from this moment I am at war with the whole world.

GLAD. Well, if I must, though I assure you I shall treasure up these brief moments of our conversation as the happiest of my existence. Au revoir.   [*Exit.*

CAR. (*Sotto voce.*). Go, unsuspecting youth, thy doom is sealed.

BEAT. (L.) Here you are, mother, and you too, Lord Mandeville. This is gallant indeed. Have you forgotten ?—the next is our dance.

MAN. Did Romeo forget his Juliet? Mrs. Churchill, will we not proceed together to the ball-room ?

CAR. (*Sotto voce.*) This is my last chance—now or never ! (*Crosses down* L. *of* BEATRICE. *Loud.*) I hope I don't intrude. Miss Beatrice, I have awaited this opportunity all evening. Can I offer you my arm ?

BEAT. Certainly, sir ; both, if you choose, though I am very sorry to say I cannot accept. I am engaged for this dance.

CAR. Then I shall just put my name down for the next.

BEAT. Excuse me, my list is full.

CAR. Won't you give me any chance at all ?

BEAT. You should have applied earlier, sir. I'm not to be kept for a reserve. (*To* MANDEVILLE.) The sets are forming ; let us go in.

CAR. But allow me—

MAN. Don't you see the young lady will have nothing to do with you ? How dare you be so persistent ? (*Gets between the two ladies and offers his arms.*)

CAR. Remember, uncle, you are speaking to a reputable person.

MAN. (*Scornfully.*) For whom I've paid some very disreputable debts. I drop you, sir, to sink to the level to which you belong.   [*Exit with ladies,* L. U. E.

CAR. (C.) The poet Burns once distended upon the great advantage it would be to us, to see ourselves as others see us. I don't see the point. I know that whenever people have volunteered to explain to me the light in which they saw me, I never had particular reasons to feel grateful for their kindness. I think it best not to know what others think about us. Human happiness consists mainly in ignoring defects. What matters the lack of wealth if we feel not the want of it ? or what the luxuries we do not miss ? There is nothing so cruel in reverses, if they do not jar against susceptibilities ; and that misfortune only is to be pitied which, if not painful, still worries its sensitive victim. I don't care now if I have to remain a bachelor, for I think that love is a sham. How many have made the observation that a clergyman, a year, and a baby generally suffice to dispel all the romance there is in love. After marriage kisses grow stale, lodge nights come into play, and the rhapsodies that erst did charm the lover's ear, now only serve to drown the midnight mewlings of incipient belles and beaux. Here comes that puppy Gladwold. I shall wreak on him my righteous rage. Oh ! I shall get even with him.

[*Enter* GLADWOLD, L. 2 E.]

GLAD. (L.) Hallo, Prentiss ! what are you doing here ? —-wasting your most valuable time. Don't be sulky ; shake, old boy. .(*Takes* CARRINGTON'S *hand.*)

CAR. I always like to shake the hand of a sensible man.

GLAD. Ah, thank you ! thank you !

CAR. And I grieve to say that on this occasion my desire is not gratified.

GLAD. Oh ! that's a joke. Ha ! ha ! By the way, old boy, did you notice that American girl Miss Hastings ?—isn't that her name ? Jupiter, ain't she a beauty ?

CAR. I have noticed you hanging to Miss Churchill's side all evening, looking for all the world just like a poodle-dog.

GLAD. I say, this is too much. I don't want you to confound me with a poodle-dog.

CAR. All right ; I confound you without the poodle-dog.

GLAD. That will do ; say no more. I accept your apology. I know every feller feels a little touchy when he is afraid another feller will cut him out with a young lady. Let's go empty a bottle wine. That'll cheer you up a bit, old boy. (*Drawing him on.*)

CAR. I'm bound to be thwarted at every turn.
                    [*Exeunt both*, L. 2. E.

[*Enter* ROBERT *and* DORA, L. U. E.]

ROB. Come, Dora, let us rest here awhile ; my brain's awhirl and my head sways as with the motion of the leader's baton.

DORA. (L.) I am proud of you, cousin, moving like a king among the whole assemblage. I did not think that in America you could have time to keep in burnish all the social arts that you have displayed to-night.

ROB. Leave compliments to the vain. See, I hold you far above such flattery. When conversation's source gives out, praise comes readiest to the tongue. We are prone to use it far too wantonly, and much abuse has made it meaningless. Let us forget the ball-room for a moment ; there are some pictures of the past now in my mind, in which you share. You cannot remember them.

DORA. Oh, but I do, though memory dimly still reflects them. I was seven years old when you left, and could retain impressions.

ROB. Do you remember how you followed me wherever I went ?

DORA. You must have studied botany at the time, for then you awed me with those strange names you gave to the wild plants and common herbs that grow profusely in our fields.

ROB. And since then fifteen years have left their print upon me.

DORA. How time flies !

ROB. Time flies ? Not so, cousin ! not so ! Time stays ! 'Tis we alone that go. The hours that strike mark but the measure of our lives. If youth does feel itself immortal, we soon perceive the bounds of our horizon, and maturity already lies in the shadow of the night that must end all. Like summer fruit, we ripen only to decay.

DORA. This is a sad philosophy to teach. Pray heaven, what would become of us if we all took such sombre, melancholy views of life.

ROB. You are right, Dora ; it is an evil mood that leads to such deep thoughts. We only mar our peace of mind do we dissect existence and view with cynic eyes the brief delusive pleasures it affords. For like the painted scenes and trappings of the stage, we break the charm if we do scan too closely. When deception flies the zest of life goes with it.

DORA. No doubt all ends the same. Then isn't it a pity that we can't make of our short existence one round of pleasure and enjoyment?

ROB. Not so; we'd tire of day were it to last too long. So constant ease and constant flowers and smiling skies harmonize into monotony and lull to sleep the better, wilder, grander portions of our nature. But hark! the music ceases and the dance is over. We shall be disturbed here, and I have some things yet to tell you. Let us retire toward that recess yonder. (*Both walk toward* R..U. E.)

[*Enter* MARGARET, L. U. E.]

MAR. There he goes with that imperious beauty whose studied welcome has strangely chilled me through and through. I cannot control this restlessness. What makes my heart so heavy? See how he stands there oblivious of all but her beside him!

[*Enter* REGINALD, L. 2 E., *with bouquet*.]

REG. (L.) Why, Margaret, I have been looking for you everywhere. See this bouquet I have brought you —fresh plucked and bound.

MAR. (R. *Not noticing* REGINALD. *Low.*) How affectionately he bends over her!

REG. Now this is cruel, Margaret; you do not even thank me for this gift I took such trouble to procure.

MAR. I am sure I appreciate the present very much.

REG. How constrainedly you speak! Have I offended you?

MAR. Oh no.

REG. I declare, Margaret, you look pale; your hand trembles in my grasp.

MAR. (*Aside*.) I fear my feelings have betrayed me.

REG. Let me lead you to this chair. Tell me what is the matter?

MAR. Nothing! a slight dizziness from dancing. I shall soon be better.

REG. I'll call mother in.

MAR. I beg of you send no one.   I had rather be left alone   Please go.

REG. I see you want to get rid of me.   Well, have it as you wish.   [*Exit* REGINALD, L. U. E.

MAR. I am sorry I sent him away.   I am not fit for the ball-room yet, or I would follow him.   (*Goes up.*) Still there?   I must compose myself.   (*Stands leaning against chair down* L.)

ROB. (*To* DORA *in background.*)   It was my father's wish that brought me back to England and to you.   Tell me, have I come too late?

MAR. How fervently he speaks, yet not a word can I distinguish.   Oh, I cannot avert my eyes..

ROB. My sole ambition was the fulfilment of his one dying hope.   I tried to make myself worthy of you, and see, of all my father's heritage I have relinquished everything but you.

MAR. He clasps her to him.   Oh!   (*Chair falls.* ROBERT *and* DORA *come forward.*)

ROB. (C.)   Margaret! weeping!   Has any one in this house dared to offend you?

MAR. (L.)   No! no!   (*Sobbing.*)

ROB. There, compose yourself.   I left you in charge of Reginald.   Where is he?

DORA. The poor girl is shy.   Don't weep, dear.   Tell me what ails you.   The company is strange to her and the excess of new emotions find their vent in tears.

[*Enter* REGINALD, L. U. E.]

ROB. Reginald, what does this mean?   How came Margaret to be here alone?

REG. I have just returned for her.   She complained of dizziness and begged me to leave her here awhile.

DORA. All this only excites her more.   Neither of you can be of service here.   The guests will remark our absence.   Better go in while I remain with her.

ROB. Shall I leave you, Margaret?

MAR. Please do.

ROB. (*To* REGINALD.)   Well, then, come.   Are you sure no one has offended her?

REG. Do you think I would allow it?

[*Exeunt both*, L. U. E.

DORA. So, my lady, you have been playing the eaves-dropper. I have suspected you, and now detected you. You may well lie there and hide your confusion in affected tears. Oh! (*Enter* CARRINGTON, L. U. E.) you need not answer, for your guilt is plain.

CAR. (*Sotto voce.*) Hallo! what's up now I wonder. My lady postures like a vengeful Amazon.

DORA. I'll feed your jealousy. Robert has offered me his heart, which I can accept or spurn just as I choose. What secret link is there between you that you should dog his footsteps like a spy. Are you so hardened that you can brave all shame, all modesty, by giving public exhibition of your passion for a man who keeps you near him but on sufferance. Tell me, I insist; for I have a right to know, what is, what has Robert Churchill been to you?

CAR. (*Stepping between them.*) As I notice the young lady addressed is not now in position to answer, I shall make bold to explain that Mr. Robert Churchill is, was, or has been Miss Hasting's guardian legal and otherwise.

DORA. I did not know, sir, that you were listening.

CAR. Nothing I have heard can lower my estimation of your ladyship in the least.

DORA. Mr. Carrington, this is impertinent, and if I choose—

CAR. To commit those trifling breaches upon ordinary hospitality, it is certainly wrong of a mere guest to spoil such hilarious freaks.

[*Enter* MRS. CHURCHILL, BEATRICE, *and* MANDEVILLE. BEATRICE *runs over to where* MARGARET *is kneeling with her head buried in a sofa.*]

MRS. C. (R. *of* DORA.) Dora, my dear, this is neglecting your duties as a hostess. I must certainly reprove you. Good gracious, what is the meaning of this scene? No one answers. Will not you speak, Mr. Carrington?

CAR. (C.) Oh, it is nothing—a little dispute.

MRS. C. A dispute? What was it?

CAR. About titles and nobility.

Mrs. C. What has Miss Hastings to do with nobility ? I never heard of such a thing as rank in America.

Car. But they have a title that all respect and venerate, which in itself means more than countess, marchioness, duchess, princess, or even queen.

Mrs. C. And what is that ?

Car. Just what Miss Hastings is—a lady.

Man. The boy is absolutely mad.

END OF ACT II.

ACT III.

SCENE—*Room in* CHURCHILL'S *house.   Door in flat and set door in* L. 2 E.   *A writing-desk and large arm-chair,* R. 2 E., *and several chairs at back.*   ROBERT *discovered seated at desk.*

Rob. Five thousand pounds all squandered within six months ! What a fortune that once would have seemed to me ! My agent writes me from London that he could contest the debt, which, while it would lay bare the villain, would not save Reginald from disgrace. I gave Reginald to understand that it would be impossible for me to give the entire sum. Yet if he could so manage as to postpone the note due in a week, arrange it in part payments, say at three, or six, or nine, or twelve months' or two years' interval, I could—that is, I thought I could—perhaps I would be able to assist him. And in this wise I mean to scourge him with suspense and make his conscience whip him back into the proper road.

[Enter REGINALD, door flat.]

Reg. Good morning, brother.

Rob. Good morning, Reginald. (*Looks at his watch.*) Nine o'clock and you up already. What is the matter ? Have you turned over a new leaf ? Come, you are forgetting the *rôle* of a young aristocrat.

Reg. (L.) Always the cynic. When will you commence thinking me capable of something serious. Once

I'm out of this scrape, I'll show you what sort of a man I am.

Rob. What sort of a man ? Why, of the sort that all men are, brought up as you have been. I have heard of a certain lordling, to whom idleness became so distasteful that if he lost one day's work he couldn't do anything for a week to get over it. (*Laughing.*)

Reg. Laugh, if you please. I sha'n't resent your sarcasms now. It will be different some time. I have been planning out a new career for myself.

Rob. Yes, and you will be kept so busy planning that you won't have time to accomplish anything. You are too ready with your promises. Don't grow impatient ; I know you have come for a purpose. Well, proceed ; what is it ?

Reg. You know as well as I do what is in my mind. The debt troubles me ; I am sick and worried ; and yet you talk as if you took no interest in me at all.

Rob. I said I would assist you all I can ; and do you think by that I would deprive myself of what I need to help you play the squanderer ?

Reg. I thought you were rich—as rich as Crœsus.

Rob. Who told you so ? And were I rich, and were that money but a tittle of my fortune, I would not pay the debt. The sin that you are guilty of should not be so easily condoned ; where rebuke is the only interdiction vice grows arrogant and strong.

Reg. But the thing is done. What shall I do ?

Rob. I will try to help you ; only let this matter rest, and give me time to work it out. By the way, how is it all his letters are addressed in my name, to Robert Churchill ?

Reg. Oh, that is easily explained. They all call me Bob at college and in London, and so he naturally supposed that my name is Robert. Then I can count on your assistance ?

Rob. As I have told you, yes.

Reg. There is something else that has awakened in me the desire to improve myself. It is but lately that I have felt it, and it has stolen over me slowly and unawares. I'll make a confident of you. Brother, I am in love with Margaret.

Rob. (*Restrainedly.*) I have noticed it.

Reg. You seem displeased.

Rob. And Margaret returns your love?

Reg. What though her heart be free, with your consent and everything in my favor should I not win her?

Rob. (*Slowly.*) Why should you not? Why should you not?

Reg. How you look at me. Do you object? I shall make myself worthy of her. I'll prove to you that I have that within me—

Rob. There, that will do. I know what you would say. Leave me now. I have a great deal to do.

Reg. Not before you promise that you won't disparage me with Margaret.

Rob. I won't. Now go. (*Exit* Reginald, *door flat.*) I must find him worthy of her ere I can commit the prize to him. At some time I must relinquish her. What is in that that I should dread so much? I had best leave that strain, for it brings thoughts I feel ashamed to own. Why is it that when all nature seems pandering to our taste, we surfeit of its blessings? We have ease and court trouble; we have sufficient, yet crave excess. Each wish fulfilled bears some new wish more fiercely sought, much harder to be reached. Still will we make ourselves unhappy by striving for what we cannot have, or sigh for that which 'twere better not to gain. I have looked forward to this meeting with Dora as yearns the soul for paradise. Her love was my life's dream. Yet now that I seem to have attained it I do not feel the joy I thought I would, and every nearer step to her, in stronger outline brings another picture to my mind. (*Enter* Mrs. Churchill, l. 2 e.) Good morning, mother. When did you come in?

Mrs. C. Just now. Are you busy?

Rob. Have you anything to tell me?

Mrs. C. Yes.

Rob. Something to interest me?

Mrs. C. Something that concerns you.

Rob. Take this cozy arm-chair. Never mind. I'll draw up another seat. Now, what is it?

Mrs. C. When your poor father died leaving me with less than moderate means, I strove hard and endured everything for my children, in the hope that they would some day repay me for my care, and make my old age happy in their honor and prosperity.

Rob. All of which I trust will be fulfilled.

Mrs. C. While you had separated yourself from us, and found your fortune in another country, I believed that the future and prestige of our family in England rested upon Reginald, and hoped that if I could secure him some rich and influential alliance he could gain a field for his capabilities, and shed new lustre upon our decaying house.

Rob. So instead of spurring him to work his way up by his own endeavors, you want him to marry rich, and forfeit his manliness and self-esteem for a dependent ease and unrespected honors? How plausible an interested tongue can make the meanest acts appear! Here is fortune-hunting made to look respectable.

Mrs C. You forget, Robert, that this is not America, and it is almost impossible for a young man without means to gain the foothold of success.

Rob. Well, and what is the drift of all this?

Mrs. C. Simply that with your arrival an obstacle has arisen that threatens to upset my hopes, and spoil Reginald's career.

Rob. Be more plain. What do you mean?

Mrs. C. I am displeased with the attention Reginald is paying to Margaret. I fear—

Rob. Be careful, mother; Margaret is my ward, and even from you I will not brook a word against her.

Mrs. C. But remember her lineage and ours.

Rob. Her father left her an untarnished name. What more could he do?

Mrs. C. (*Sneeringly.*) An actor's daughter!

Rob. An actor's daughter! The indignity lies in the reproach, not in the expression. A good actor is a good preacher, and his pulpit is the stage. Not so pretentious as he that is ordained, yet often more effective. There's a religion, mother, one cannot learn in church—a charity no doctrine can convey. At the theatre, those temples to human genius built, we learn at first all that the tender heart may feel and bear, the height to which the soul can soar. And those who minister at that shrine, who

of themselves can make the faithful picture of some great
mind's dream, may well lay claim to our respect—to all
the dignity of art.

MRS. C. I did not intend to disparage the man, nor
his profession. You force me to speak plainly. I have
seen enough of aspiring poverty, and if I have my way,
when Reginald marries, he will marry rich.

ROB. (*Aside.*) Ah, ha ! I should have known as
much : all that is meant by lineage, pride, ambition, the
foothold of success—all that means money. (*Loud.*)
Margaret is an heiress. She will inherit a valuable estate.

MRS. C. I thought her father died indigent.

ROB. Not all actors die poor. Her father in his time
was immensely rich—(*aside*) in hopes. Poor fellow, he left
scarce means enough to bury him.

MRS. C. I never heard a word of this.

ROB. That is because the property is all entered in my
name, in trust for her.

MRS. C. Poor girl ! I have been mistaken in her.

ROB. (*Aside.*) Mammon works wonders. I would
buy your happiness, Margaret, even at the cost of my
own. (*Loud.*) · You must excuse me now. I had forgotten an urgent transaction I have to-day in London,
and the train leaves in a few minutes. (*Arises and crosses
to* L.)

MRS. C. Dora and Lord Mandeville promised to be
here. When will you return ?

ROB. This evening.   [*Exit door in flat.*

MRS. C. (C.) There is some mystery about him. Is
he rich or poor ? He never speaks about himself. All
that I know is that he lives well and spends his money
freely. I can't understand what there was that so disturbed him in that message he received the day of his
arrival here. (*Looks over desk.*) I am sure he has taken
Reginald in his confidence, yet I cannot get a word from
him either. I have ferreted his papers every opportunity
I had, but could discover nothing. Still, I am convinced
there is something wrong. (*Picks up a letter.*) Let me
see what this is ? (*Reads.*) " Mr. Robert Churchill :
You have delayed me too long with idle excuses. I refuse to be deceived any longer. If you try, you can
easily obtain the money from your relatives, and unless

you do so you will compel me to proceed against you. I can have you condemned in any country to which you may escape. Remember you have obtained the money from me through your fraudulent pretensions to an estate which I have since discovered to be yours only in name. I only wait until this matter is settled to return to America, and must see you at once on receipt of this. (signed) Thomas Wrexford." Why that is just what Robert told me ; now my suspicions are confirmed. Ah ! who comes here ? (*Hides letter.*)

[*Enter* MARGARET, L. 2 E.]

MAR. (L.) Is Robert here ?

MRS. C. (R.) No ; he has just left for London. (MARGARET *turns to go.*) Stay a moment.

MAR. Have you anything to tell me, Mrs. Churchill ?

MRS. C. You should not be so shy of me, my child. I wanted to tell you I am sorry to see you have taken Dora's hasty words of that night to heart.

MAR. It is not easy to forget.

MRS. C. Yet now that she has confessed herself in the wrong and asked your forgiveness, you should not repel her advances.

MAR. I do not, Mrs. Churchill, though in truth I would rather avoid them. I will not willingly come in her way again.

MRS. C. Don't say that, for you may grow to like her yet. You see love is always suspicious, and under like circumstances women are apt to make some foolish trifle the cause for jealousy.

MAR. The proud and beautiful Lady Percival jealous of a poor orphan girl ? Oh no !

MRS. C. Not as poor as you say, nor as unpretentious as you think. I know your affection for Robert is as pure as it is sincere. You are ignorant of the world, my child, and don't know what little will give rise to evil thoughts.

MAR. That is so, Mrs. Churchill, though I doubted it before. Lady Dora has more right to Robert than I. I shall try hard—very hard—to school myself, and not let my gratitude and actions toward him ever offend her again.

Mrs. C. That is a noble resolution. Keep yourself distant as propriety demands. See here comes some one who loves you more sincerely than ever Robert did.

[*Enter* Reginald, *door in flat.*]

Reg. (l. *of* Margaret.) Here you are ! Now this is a neat way to do. I've had the horses saddled these two hours for the gallop you wanted to take with me this morning.

Mar. I did not promise to go. I told you I would consider it, and I had rather —

Reg. Tush, tush ! I can't afford to let you off this time, my lady. The fields look so green and the weather is so inviting, that I really am impatient to be out. Besides, I know what you can do on horseback, and I am just in the humor to try your skill.

Mrs. C. Don't refuse him, my dear. The exercise will do you good. Come, I'll help you on with your riding habit. (*Crosses with* Margaret *to door* l. 2 e.)

Mar. Well, if I must.

Reg. Why certainly you must. [*Exeunt all*, l. 2 e.

[*Enter* Carrington *and* Beatrice, *door in flat.*]

Beat. (r.) Let me tell you, sir, I don't believe a word of what you say. Why didn't you come to me the night of the ball instead of leaving me to flirt with anybody that would only favor you with a glance ?

Car. (l.) But won't you listen ?

Beat. Not one word, sir ! I'm not the one to be flattered and cajoled when the humor offers, only to be slighted at pleasure.

Car. I would only be too happy to think that you care for my attention.

Beat. Indeed ; then I shall make you happy by letting you know that I care to have your attention directed toward others. So you let me alone.

Car. I would creep into the furthermost corners of the earth if I knew you desired it.

Beat. Oh ! that would be unnecessary. I believe I could feel myself very comfortable, even if I knew you were barely out of sight.

Car. And is it thus you slight my affection ? I have

laid my heart at your feet and you ruthlessly trample upon it. Yet though your sentence be the crushing of my hopes, the funeral knell to my ambition, and though your undeserved treatment fret me to an early grave, yet, oh, thrice cruel beauty ! can I bear thee no resentment, and dying bless thee still.

BEAT. Young man, you waste your talents here. Try it on elsewhere. You may find some one more susceptible.

CAR. Since that confounded uncle of mine came unto this house, my influence is spoiled.

BEAT. Don't swear, sir ! What have I to do with your uncle ?

CAR. You don't pretend to be ignorant of his intentions, do you ?

BEAT. I don't know anything about his intentions, and they don't concern you. He has better manners than you have.

CAR. What ! you would compare that old eccentric skinflint with me ?

BEAT. You should be ashamed to speak in that way of your uncle, sir.

CAR. Haven't I a right to speak of my own uncle as I please ? But I say, Beatrice, you can't really be in earnest to listen to the old cad ; he is three or four times your age, gray as a bat, and was a thriving candidate for baldheadtorial honors ever since I knew him. Do be . reasonable, won't you ? It seems that your aversion is to me like the North Pole—I can never get around it. The more I try to please you, the less you like me for it.

BEAT. That is because you deserve it. What have you ever done that I should treat you otherwise. Such impromptu pleadings as you make are never sincerely meant.

CAR. Shall I give it to you in writing—so that there's no mistake about it ?

BEAT. Well, that might be better if it were poetry, for instance.

CAR. Oh, poetry, I've written lots of it in my time. I know a particular poem, one that took me I know not how long to plan ; one week to write, another week to arrange it, and a whole month to get it to a perceptible rhyme.   I haven't had time to attend to the metre yet.

BEAT. Let me have it.

CAR. You won't mind if you find your name mixed up in it ?

BEAT. Not too much.

CAR. Just a little ?

BEAT. Well.

CAR. It commences—now I'm not sure that I have it properly memorized. But that does not make much difference. You see it is of the kind of poems wherein those parts that are left out are always best appreciated. And to show you how anxious I am to gratify you, I shall abstain from inflicting any of it upon you. See what great sacrifices I am willing to make for you.

BEAT. How very considerate ! But you have excited my curiosity. Just recite a portion of it.

CAR. Well.

> The ice is cold, the sun is hot,
> The rose is red, but the lily is not.
> On the contrary, it is white.
> Oh dost thou then my love requite ?

> Joy is not joy, nor is bliss bliss
> Where thou art not, when thy sweet face I miss
> I feel as it were dejected.
> Art thou—art thou likewise—affected—

Affected—that doesn't fit in there quite, does it ? but then it rhymes amazingly. Now some people might object because the sense is a little obscure ; but you see we poets don't look to that at all—the rhyme is the main question. Shall I continue ?

BEAT. Do you know any more like that ?

CAR. A great deal more.

BEAT. And will you recite it all now ?

CAR. Yes, certainly, if you like.

BEAT. How long will it take you ?

CAR. About an hour or so.

BEAT. Dear me, how apropos ; this will just give me sufficient time to finish my sewing in the arbor. Be sure you get done by the time I come back. Au revoir.

[Exit door in flat.

CAR. My effort has certainly had an astonishing effect. Verily the world's a stage, and the most of us are crushed tragedians.   When next I attempt poetry it will be when I can rhyme my name with donkey.   Hallo! here is something for good measure.   I suppose—

[*Enter* LORD MANDEVILLE, *door in flat.*]

MAN. Well, sir, what are you doing here?   Why do you dog my footsteps?

CAR. (R.) This is a case of mistaken identity.   I didn't dog your footsteps; as it happens, I was here before you.

MAN. (L.) Not a word from you, sir.   How many times have I told you not to speak to me at all?

CAR. Just as many times as I have told you that I wouldn't if you'll only let me alone.

MAN. I would not for the world have it known to strangers, but I will tell you, sir, confidentially speaking, that you are a scoundrel—a deep-dyed scoundrel.

CAR. Confidentially speaking, you have told me all that before.   If you've nothing new to say, I humbly take my leave.   (*About to go.*)

MAN. Stay, sir; where are you going? whose home do you now intend to darken? how many new hearts do you intend to desolate?

CAR. Oh, three or four or more, just as I happen to feel about it.

MAN. You cool, unblushing villain!   I'll take good care you do no damage here.   I'll show them the degenerate rascal that you are, and they shall shun you as they would poison or the cholera.

CAR. All right.   Go ahead.   I'll see what I can do to retaliate.

MAN. The next time you get in debt, I'll see you rot in prison before I spend a farthing to help you out.

CAR. That's a good point.   Good-by.

MAN. Come, what will you take to leave this house at once and forever?

CAR. Oh, very little—if I can take the girl I love with me.   If not, the tenure and fee-simple of this earth and of all the planets that make up the universe would not buy me.. (*Looks defiant while* MANDEVILLE *shakes his fist at him.*)

END OF ACT III.

ACT IV.

SCENE—*Centre door chamber. A piano on the* L. *with lamp upon it. A table* R. U. E., *and arm-chair ; window* R. 2 E.

[*Enter* LORD MANDEVILLE *and* MRS. CHURCHILL, C. *door* L.]

MAN. (R. C.) I tell you, Mrs. Churchill, your daughter does not take kindly to me. I understand philosophy, have some knowledge of the classics, and in all departments of science I can take it up with most men. But when it comes to dealing with women I find myself " Lucus a non lucendo"—a light that does not shine.

MRS. C. (L. C.) You must not lose patience. Beatrice is only a young girl, and needs to be humored and flattered.

MAN. Not of the slightest use, madam. I have courted her by heart, and I have courted her by book. I have tried her in mathesis, with a trifling of geology for a flavor. I have spiced my conversation with a few edifying hints on the latest astronomical developments, and wound up with a sprightly and fanciful dissertation on protoplasms and evolution—but all to no avail.

MRS. C. You must try some language less profound and more sentimental.

MAN. Oh, I have sagacity enough to understand that. Why madam, the sweetest and most sympathetic passages from the entire gamut of poets. from Virgil down to Byron, won't move her. She absolutely refuses to be impressed or edified.

MRS. C. But compliments and sentiments are only effective when they are original.

MAN. Are not all compliments original ? What mat-

ter in whose words we express them, as long as the sentiments are our own ?   We do wisely to study the poets,
for the proper and more drastic utterance of our deepest
thoughts.

MRS. C. You must not be so easily discouraged.   If
you manage her rightly you may yet be successful.

MAN. I hope so, I hope so, Mrs. Churchill.

[*Enter* DORA *and* BEATRICE, C. *door* L.]

DORA (L. C.)   How beautiful your garden looks,
aunty.   I have been strolling with Beatrice around the
grounds until it was too dark to see.   Those lovely
acacias that were scarcely budding when I was here last,
are now in full bloom, and emit a delightful fragrance.
Ah ! here is his truant lordship.   This is gallantry, indeed, to leave us two ladies go out unprotected and alone
without even making the offer of an escort.

MAN. (R.)   Ah ! Lady Dora, you are too severe—
upon my word you are.   Do you think that I would
willingly forego the sight of the roses in their bloom or
the company of ladies when they are young and beautiful ?

DORA. Your lordship's flatteries would tempt me to
forgive, had not painful experience previously convinced
me of their insincerity.   I dread to think what mischief
your lordship's enticing ways and insinuating words must
have done to more confiding souls.

MAN. Yes, I will admit that they have done no end
of mischief—to myself.   I have never set out to captivate
anybody yet without discovering in the end that I was
the solitary victim.   King Crœsus was surprised when
the Persian Cyrus routed his forces, because the oracles
had prophesied that when he crossed the river Halys, a
great empire would be overthrown—it never struck him
until then, it was his own they meant.   And so do I,
seeking to win another's heart, play havoc with mine own.

DORA. How beautifully expressed. Beatrice, what do
you say to Lord Mandeville's last sally ?

BEAT. (L.) Oh, very fine indeed !   What was it ?

MAN. (*To* MRS. CHURCHILL.)   See, she doesn't pay
me the slightest attention.

MRS. C. (R. C.)   Dora, I have something to impart to
you.

DORA. What is it, aunty?

MRS. C. I will tell you privately. Your lordship will excuse us.

MAN. Regretfully, but resignedly.

DORA. I am loth to leave you alone. Beatrice, don't mind a word he says. His lordship is very deceitful. Oh! I know him of old. I am with you, aunty.

[*Exit with* MRS. CHURCHILL, C. *door* L.

[BEATRICE *sits down to piano* L., *and commences to play softly and hum.*]

MAN. (*Awkwardly after a pause.*) Sing, sing, sweet siren, sing! while I, more ardent than was ancient Ulysses, fall a ready victim to your alluring strains. (*Pause.*) I like music, simple, sweet, yet soul-inspiring music. Miss Beatrice, don't you like simple, sweet, yet soul-inspiring music?

BEAT. Yes.

MAN. Do you know what I think?

BEAT. No, your lordship, I do not know what you think.

MAN. Your playing just reminded me of the idea that there must be some relation between a nice picture, a statue or a person, and a fine strain of music. I wonder if anybody has ever studied the affinity of the cadences with, or the indirect derivation of the harmony of sound to the harmony of color, and—

BEAT. No, I don't know anything about that, and I don't care to, either. If your lordship like, you can take this book; there is a treatise all about it. I am sure it will amuse and interest you very much. I know it will, because I have found it too tedious for me to attempt. Just take that table yonder; I will order you a lamp.

[*Exit* C. *door* L.

MAN. (*Shouts after her.*) Don't trouble yourself on my account. (*Sotto voce.*) I half suspect that this was meant for my dismissal. Damn me if I couldn't admire her tricks, if they were not directed against myself.

[*Exit* C. R.

[*Enter* DORA *and* MRS. CHURCHILL, C. *door* L.]

MRS. C. (L.) This letter that I have read to you

proves Robert to be no more than a gambler.   He comes back to force himself into good terms with his family, and then obtain their assistance to pay his pressing debts and retrieve his fortunes.   It pains me to say this of my step son, yet duty compels me to expose him, and warn you before it is too late.

DORA (R.) And yet Robert does not appear like an adventurer.   His actions have been always proud and generous.

MRS. C. Such natures are the easiest enticed.

DORA. But Robert is just from America, and had not lingered in London a day before he came here.   How is it possible that he could have contracted there such heavy debts ?

MRS. C. Don't you see.   This Thomas Wrexford is an American.   He pursued him hither to collect the debt.   He writes he is waiting for the money to return again.   That establishes his guilt.

DORA. Is it not likely that it is meant for Reginald ? I have heard some queer rumors of his doings in London.

MRS. C. Absurd !   Reginald is barely out of college, and I at least should know his vices.   There, it is in plain letters to Mr. Robert Churchill.   Does that admit of doubt ?

DORA. Though all this be true, still I believe I can respect—yes, love him.   There are few men whose actions will bear close scrutiny.   There is something in Robert's demeanor and unpresuming dignity I cannot help admire.   What if he has nothing now ?   With me to urge him on he could soon gain that position which by right of power and genius belongs to him.   But I am glad you told me this, as I may use this fact to bend him to my will.   I'll make him set adrift this beggar he has brought with him, or make him choose twixt her and me.

[*Enter* ROBERT, C. *door* R.]

ROB. (C.) Why, mother—Dora—here in the dark ? Let me turn up the light—so.   You're not angry with me for being late ?   I was delayed, but managed with great diligence to make the last train.

MRS. C. What kept you in London ?

Rob. Business ; nothing else, I assure you, could have kept me so long away.

Mrs. C. What business, Robert, have you in London, that takes you there so often ?

Rob. You are inquisitive, mother.

Mrs. C. Why should I not know ? Is there anything in these visits that you must conceal, that you are ashamed to own ?

Rob. There is nothing I am ashamed to own, but there are some things I do not think advisable to tell. I had rather not talk about this.

Dora. See what interest your mother takes in you.

Rob. And do you too, Dora ?

Dora. Well, yes—a little.

Rob. What ! only a little. This is poor progress. I must do better and you must show me how.

Dora. Then 'tis easily done ; you have but to grant one favor that I ask.

Rob. A favor. Is that all ? Speak out, and it is done.

Dora. And you will promise what I ask ?

Rob. What can you ask that would injure me, that any man of honor and in love would or should not do ?

Dora. Then, Robert Churchill, if you do care for my love, you must send this girl away.

Rob. Who ?

Dora. Margaret Hastings.

Rob. Where ?

Dora. Anywhere, so she is out of my sight.

Rob. You cannot mean that, Dora. You would not have me drive out ruthlessly into the world this orphan, bound to my care by the holiest of promises made at her father's dying bed ?

Dora. Her presence is unbearable to me.

Rob. What cause have you ? why do you hate her ?

Dora. I hate her, because I hate her. I fear her pretty face and unctuous, hesitating tongue. Because I know while she is near I never can be complete mistress of your heart. Oh, I can be generous too, and forgiving even to my enemies—that is, those whom I can crush at will ; but I can brook no rival, and where I have cause for envy I have cause to hate.

Rob. I am sorry for you, Dora. Where malice rests there is no happiness ; the soul but clouds itself with the evil it conceives. Do you think that it will make you light and glad of heart to know that you have made another's sad and heavy ?

Dora. What a saintly and shocked expression you put on ! Come, you will never do to play the moralist. Your past spoils the effect. I know your history too well.

Rob. You are raving, Dora ; I know not of what you speak.

Dora. (*Sarcastically.*) I can account for your frequent trips to London, the mysterious correspondence you take such pains to hide. Robert Churchill, your secret's out, and given to the wind. You stand here a refugee, with your fortune shattered as your reputation, and not the debtor's fate alone—the felon's cell awaits you.

Rob. Who gave this information ? (*To* Mrs. Churchill.) Was it you ?

Mrs. C. I do not deny it.

Rob. You have played the spy.

Mrs. C. Call it what you choose. And though you were my right and only child, and though it broke my heart, I would expose you if only to warn those whom you would entoil. Do you recognize this letter ? I have suspected you from the first.

Rob. No mother's instincts will make her criminate her son. You have taken the word of an outlaw, a libertine against me, without asking my defence or any man's corroboration.

Mrs. C. Don't be too sure of that. Your frequent whisperings with Reginald and his distressed appearance convinced me that he knew something about your affairs. It was only after showing him this written proof that I prevailed upon him to confess it all, and even then he begged me with tears in his eyes to make no use of it against you. (*Takes a bell.*) I shall send for him to prove the value of your denials.

[*Enter* Servant, C. *door* L. Mrs. Churchill *whispers to him and he exits* C. *door* L.]

Rob. (*Aside.*) Did he do that ?

DORA. I do not care for vindications. Why make a scene of this?

ROB. My ambition was never for wealth alone, nor was my pride fed by success; and had I failed—for who can shield the flame of fortune that flares and flickers in the current of events—what, though I'd lost my all, think you with that I'd lose my self-respect or feel inclined to hide reproachless poverty with ignoble shams? I have faced want too often, and felt its sting, but never yet was I ashamed of it. Not resting with this charge against my manhood, you must impugn my honor.

[*Enter* REGINALD; *after him*, BEATRICE, MANDEVILLE *and* CARRINGTON, C. *door* L.]

REG. You have sent for me. (*Going to* MRS. CHURCHILL, R.)

MRS. C. I want you to confirm here, in presence of all assembled, that Robert Churchill—no matter what he professes—is only an adventurer.

REG. Be quiet, mother, for heaven's sake.

MRS. C. Here is a letter from one Thomas Wrexford who, it seems, has pursued him here to England for some five thousand pounds, obtained through fraudulence and deceit.

REG. Oh, mother, mother, you know not how much you torture me.

MRS. C. Oh, you need not try to shield him now. It is too late, and he has forced me to this step.

REG. My God! what shall I do?

ROB. (*Low.*) What your conscience dictates. Have no fear from me. Say what you will. I would not add another pang to those that rack you now. Poor coward, I pity you. (*Turns from him*, R.)

CAR. (*Who has remained at back with* BEATRICE, *whispering.*) Don't let this weakness make a rogue of you. Speak out like a man. Be true, be wise, 'tis all the same; truth lacks of wisdom but the name. (*Steps back to* C. *door* L. BEATRICE *next door*, R.)

MRS. C. He hesitates to condemn his brother.

ROB. Enough of this.

MRS. C. Ah! ha! I thought 'twould turn out so.

ROB. (*To* MRS. CHURCHILL.) You glory in my fall,

to have me blacked and blighted before all the world. You have made my childhood sad and desolate. The budding life you should have watched and cherished, you served with coldness and neglect. The young heart you might have trained to love, to cling to you, you forced it to turn away with mistrust—aye, aversion. Where you might have planted flowers to blossom, and in their ripening beauty give you richest thanks again, you sowed but pain and tears. It was you that estranged and forced me from my home. And now I have come back to say to you—my father's second wife—for his, for his hallowed memory's sake, let us be friends at last. You have accepted the proffered truce only to violate it. You have grovelled in the churchyard of the past, and brought to light what it had been best for you to have left below. I'll leave your house to-morrow.

[*Enter* MARGARET, C. *door* L.]

DORA. I will forget everything. (*Goes to him.*)

ROB. (*Disregarding* DORA, *goes up to* MARGARET.) Have you listened to all this ? These little rankling burrs that malice here throws out are scarcely worth our while to tread upon. What do I care if those who do not know speak ill of me ? But you act so strangely. Why do you turn away your head ? Has your mind been poisoned against me too ? Oh no, it is not possible— the very doubt defames you. I do not chide you, Margaret ; don't weep. I am only pained, not angry. There, there, go—gc. (MRS. CHURCHILL *leading* MARGARET *away door* C. L.)

MRS. C. I'll take you to your room, and explain his wicked conduct. · [*Exit.*

DORA (R.) There is the guileless and confiding nature whom you have reared and cared for all her life. Lord Mandeville, it is getting late ; will you attend me home ?

MAN. (*Who is standing at the table,* R.) Presently, your ladyship, presently. [*Exit* DORA, C. *door* R.

BEAT. (*Going up to* ROBERT.) Brother,, I don't believe a word of anything said against you. Moreover, I believe you can clear this up any time you choose. But I do suspect that you now refuse to vindicate yourself, because you are too noble to do so by getting anybody else into trouble. Now please, Robert, don't take mother's words too much to heart. I am sure that she must feel some inkling of the truth, which irritates her all the more. Let her find out how cruelly unjust she was, and you will see, it will hurt her more than you, and she will do anything for reparation.

ROB. You are a noble girl, Beatrice.

BEAT. Good night.

ROB. Good night. [*Exit* BEATRICE C. *door* L.

MAN. Sir, I have been an unwilling witness to an unpleasant scene. Yet I assure you, sir, you stand not less for it in my regard. I have taken a liking to you, Mr. Churchill, and have found nothing in your character but what I must sanction and admire. If now—pardon the presumption—you are suffering the effects of some little indiscretion, I beg that you will not hesitate to accept my assistance. Whatever you need, call on me. Don't be backward. I ask it as a favor. Call on me at any time. (*Turns round and faces* CARRINGTON, C., *who is advancing, stares at him for a moment, and then walks off as if in disgust,* C. *door* R.)

CAR. Mr. Churchill, allow me to grasp your hand ; you are a gentleman. Good-night. [*Exit* C. *door* R.

ROB. Good-night. (*Turns down the light, throws himself into arm-chair, and remains silent for a while with his face buried in his hands.*) Another bubble broken. Faith is a fallacy and gratitude a dream. How all experience tends to teach us selfishness. (*Rises.*) Come, cheer up, man, cheer up ; the greatest harm that people can do is to themselves. I should laugh at this. No use ! We can't philosophize with our feelings, and humor rules us against our will. What a monstrous bubble humor is ! Without a form, without a substance, changing with the wind and weather, it is the weakness of mankind, and its tyrant. It is the foe and worriment of age, the mocking sprite that holds out to us that will o' the wisp which man calls hope, then, darkening, shrouds us in despair. This peevish child of thought weighs heavy upon the heart while 'tis cradled on the brow. (*Steps to a window and looks out.*) Ah ! this is a grateful breeze. The sky is studded with stars, and not a cloud to emblemize the

misery below. 'Twas such a night as this when I left
England. Just such a moon seemed looking down with
pity upon my loneliness. How I have suffered since !
Where is the bliss I once anticipated ? Take it all in all
the past is but a mirror of the future. Storm-clouds
have passed, dark clouds must come again. Joy and
woe, and smiles and tears, like changing seasons, hold
their visits round. A birth to feast, a death to mourn,
mayhap a marriage comes between. We struggle to
reach a goal, disappointments come ; yet still we plod.
Obstacles in rugged mountains rise, and in vast deserts
intervene. Chance bears us on, or holds us back, and
while pursuing each our aim, there come gray hairs and
furrows on the brow, bent form, and palsied limbs ; and
then—and then we reach it. Reach what ? the end.
(*Footsteps are heard.*) Hark, what is that ? (*Moves
stealthily toward the* C. *door.*) Who is this ?

[*Enter* MARGARET C. *door* L.]

MAR. (L.) 'Tis I—Margaret.

ROB. (R.) What brings you here at this time ?

MAR. I could not help it, Robert. I tried in vain to
sleep, but something would not let me. You are not
angry, are you, Robert, because when this evening you
spoke to me I turned away ? Yes, cold and warily turned
away. I did it for your sake—indeed I did. I have
been told and I have found it out, that it is not right for
me to permit you to be so kind to me. That we should
be more strange and distant to each other. Dora demands it, too, and should I not do everything to please
the one whom you intend to make your wife ? And I
have heard—what it is torture for me to believe—that
you are poor—ruined. To save me pain, to hide from
me the knowledge of your losses, you have permitted me
to waste your lessening means in empty pleasures and idle
luxuries. And I accepted all you gave, because I thought
that you were rich. How could I know that every glit-
tering ornament, the costly dresses you surprised me
with, were all as blood drops from your breast. You
should have known that I must learn the truth some
day ; and then to make me feel that I, who should have
gladdened your life, have but added to its misery, and in-

stead of lightening your load have helped to weigh you down. Oh, this was cruel, Robert, so cruel. How have I deserved this from you? Here are my jewels—every one. Don't disdain them from my hand. They have cost you a great deal, and they may assist you more than you now believe. All I have is yours. I will give up everything. I will slave for you day and night, and it shall be my sole happiness to prove my gratitude. Only, Robert, leave this country. The land that rewarded your efforts once will not refuse you now — where people may be poor without being dependent, and the lowly may strive without danger of slight. See, Robert, on my knees I beg of you come back—back to America. (*Sinks on her knees.* ROBERT, *as if too overpowered to speak, kisses her forehead.*)

END OF ACT IV.

ACT V.

SCENE—*Handsome apartments.* DOORS *in flat and set doors,* R. *and* L. 2 E.

[*Enter* ROBERT *and* MANDEVILLE, *door* R. 2 E.]

MAN. (L.) So you are determined to go back again to America?

ROB. (R.) I had never intended to remain here long; besides, my business requires my presence there.

MAN. You may believe that I shall regret to see you go. You are the only man to whom I can talk a sensible word—in fact, the only man who will listen to me at all; and you do not know how much you will oblige me if in some way you would enable me to give you some testimonial of my friendship.

ROB. Then I am in a position to take advantage of your kind offer?

MAN. Well, sir, what is it?

ROB. That you sanction the match between your

nephew and my sister Beatrice. You see the two people are in love ; and what is the use of standing in their way ?

MAN. You cannot mean it, Mr. Churchill ! Do you think that for his graceless conduct I am going to let him cut me out ? I'll teach him how to worry me in the future. I may have only a small chance myself, but he shall not glory in getting her ; not if I can help it, sir.

ROB. But you must allow the girl to have her preferences ; you see she likes him.

MAN. Oh, I shall overcome that. She need not have me, but she must refuse him, too.

ROB. How can you expect that ? Everybody has a will, an instinct of their own. There are many planets whirling round the sun : each has its movements, each its orbit's swing, sways one pendulum to a clock, one mind, one frame. Surely, a man of your wisdom and experience should know that while it is possible to inspire another's thoughts, and to swerve them, we cannot enforce them, nor can we crush them.

MAN. Mr. Churchill, you have me cornered ; and if only to keep my promise to you I shall not stand in their way. But you would scarcely believe what that boy has made me suffer.

ROB. Take my word, sir, he has some good qualities in him which only require years and a little forbearance on your part to bring out. You see your harshness has only made him obdurate.

MAN. I shall take your advice, sir, though I am sure the young dog does not deserve it. They are coming. I believe I had best get out of their way. (*Retires a moment back, then exit* L. *door.*)

[*Enter* BEATRICE *and* CARRINGTON, *door* L.]

ROB. Well, where have you been ?

BEAT. (L.) Taking a stroll.

ROB. (R.) Taking a stroll ? you two?

BEAT. I'm sure it wasn't of my choosing. He would persist in following me in spite of my remonstrance.

ROB. Well, sir, what do you mean by following this lady in spite of her remonstrance ?

CAR. (C.) Oh ! she didn't remonstrate so very much ; besides, if your honor will allow me to plead before this court, I would make bold to state that the opposing counsel has not presented the case in proper form.

Rob. Allow me to be the judge of that. Continue with the prosecution. What did this objectionable person persist in telling you?

Beat. Oh, nothing.

Car. There, you see, can you find fault with that?

Rob. A great deal, sir. You should have put in your time to better advantage. You may now retire (*motioning* Carrington *away*) while I cross-examine the witness. (*Exit* Carrington, *door* L.) Why do you tease the poor fellow so? I know he loves you ardently.

Beat. How do you know that I love him?

Rob. Oh, I can see it in your eyes. Take my advice: don't be too sure of him. Think what rash things people sometimes do when they imagine their love is unrequited. He might run away or do something still worse, and you may have yet to blame yourself for blighting his existence.

Beat. I wouldn't have him do that; but I do not want him—to—to—annoy me so much. It would be wicked to blight his life, poor dear; but I sha'n't let him be too presumptive.   [*Exit door* L.

Rob. How discontent will feed on other people's happiness. I wish I could forget myself. (*Sees* Reginald *at the door* R.) Why do you stand hesitating there? Are you ashamed to face me?

Reg. (R.) How can I look you in the face after what I have done?

Rob. (L.) Don't harp upon this perpetually. I am satisfied to wipe it from my memory. Here are the papers and a receipt in full. Destroy them. Let the consuming flames burn from your mind all inclinations to such vile recklessness hereafter.

Reg. And you shower this generosity upon one who has shown himself so thankless, so base! Oh, brother!

Rob. There, there, I was as much to blame as you. I should have been more open. This will teach me as well as you—there's no security in subterfuge.

Reg. You have taught me what it is to be a man. And if my new-born spirit does not lie to me, you will yet find me worthy of your confidence.

Rob. (*Accepting* Reginald's *hand.*) I believe you.
(*As if trying to appear disinterested.*) But stay, how are
you prospering in that affair of yours, your suit for
Margaret ?

Reg. I have not had the heart to speak to her of late.
In fact, the more I consider the more I am compelled to
see how entirely unworthy I am of her.

Rob. And yet I think I have noticed that she likes
you.

Reg. I thought so, too, at one time, but now she
seems more cold and distant every day.

Rob. That is not so. You will have her yet. I cannot stay to see your marriage ; though I would like to
have this event settled before I am away—to-day. You
will find her in yonder room. See her now ; it is my desire ; I shall not listen to excuses. Go. (*Exit* Reginald,
door in flat.) And thus forever do I thrust away my
happiness. My God ! must duty always be to me a de-
privation—mine the only sacrifice. Can I do otherwise ?
I'm not so blind as to mistake her gratitude for love.
It would be selfish to bind her thus to me. How could
I enjoy what can only be affected, or perceive unmoved
the pain that she must feel to hide the truth from me.

[*Enter* Mrs. Churchill, *door l.*]

Mrs. C. (l.) May I speak a word to you ? Robert,
I cannot bear to see you go, without telling you how
bitterly I feel the humiliation .my own unworthy
suspicions have brought upon me.

Rob. (r.) But why recall what must be unpleasant to
us both ?

Mrs. C. I have treated you shamefully and unnatu-
rally, and instead of using the power for retaliation that
my injustice gave you, you have revenged yourself only
with kindness.

Rob. You only served me right for aiding to deceive
you.

Mrs. C. And the money you have laid out for Reginald—

Rob. We will let that stand to bear its interest in love.

[*Enter* MANDEVILLE, *door* L.]

MAN. (L.) It's past, the thing is done. Mrs. Churchill, you may congratulate me.

MRS. C. (C.) Did I not always say your lordship would ultimately be successful?

MAN. Did you? Well, I have been—in coming to my senses. I have discovered, madam, that for me the period of romance has slipped by. I have convinced myself that I am too old to leave my study and my books, to seek now what I had neglected in my youth. That instead of persisting in a hopeless rivalry, it were better for me to assist the winning party, and instead of sulking at my discomfiture, quiescently accept my fate; and in reaping the thanks gain at least some small share of the happiness, the bliss, to which I have assisted others.

ROB. A very sage and politic conclusion!

MAN. Oh, trust me for knowing what is right. You will always find, Mr. Churchill, that people of my age are very deliberate, and do nothing without good reasons. Only young men are hot-headed, and refuse to be convinced. You, at least, Mr. Churchill, understand me and comprehend my objects. You can value my instructions, and as you will accept nothing more material, allow me to assure you that, no matter how critical the standpoint or how delicate the question, you will always be welcome to my advice—whenever you write for it. I shall see you later. Mrs. Churchill, if you will accept my arm I shall explain it all.

[*Exeunt* MANDEVILLE *and* MRS. CHURCHILL, *door* L.

[*Enter* REGINALD, *door in flat.*]

ROB. (R.) Back already? In tears? I cannot understand this. Has Margaret refused you? You put me out of patience. Why don't you speak?

REG. (L.) Why should I, when you have already guessed the truth?

ROB. Impossible! You were too hasty—too impetuous.

REG. I did my best.

Rob. You should not have forced conclusion ; you should have given her time.

Reg. She was calm and self-possessed. And when she said that she could never be my wife, her grave, sad voice convinced me that the decision was irrevocable.

Rob. Send her to me. Tell her I wish to speak to her. (*Exit* Reginald, *door flat.*) I know she loves him. Yet she refuses him for my sake. No, no, I cannot accept the sacrifice.

[*Enter* Margaret, *door in flat.*]

Mar. (r.) You have sent for me, Robert ?

Rob. (l.) Yes, Reginald has made me the confidant of his love for you, and I wished to tell you how glad it would make me to see your future provided for. I know he loves you dearly, and will make you a good husband. You will be happy with him. I pressed him to this declaration because I wanted this matter settled before I go.

Mar. And you urged him on, thinking that my heart was as a vane that could be turned at will. You would give me away as a plaything that one grows weary of. You are tired of me, and wish me from your presence. Oh, I understand it all. Very well, it shall be as you wish. Only let me go back to my native land ; there I shall leave you, and you will never see me again. I have an aunt living somewhere in the West, whom I shall seek until I find her out. She'll not refuse to share her home with me. I shall not be a burden there. Oh, I can work, I can do many things to earn my livelihood.

Rob. There was a rare exotic blooming in a garden, and enchanted by its bold rich coloring a boy would sit by it day by day to watch the phases of its growth, and dream. There came a time when that boy had to seek in foreign lands the peace, the comfort he could not find at home. And all that gave the parting pain was this same strange plant to which in silence he had so often poured out his sorrows, and so relieved himself. And he carried its memories with him across the ocean, and through many years. But in his new abode, while he was still unfriended and alone, another flower sprang up as if to cheer him in his loneliness ; and that flower's existence became his joy ; and it.was his delight to see it blossom in all its pure and tender loveliness.   Yet did he not prize it as he should have done ; for the recollection of that gayer plant, the passion of his youth, still haunted him, until he resolved to return from whence he came to where it grew, and if possible to claim it for his own.   And when he beheld that flower again, the charm was broken, for its stately luxuriant ripeness disappointed him, and its brilliant hues repelled him by their very gorgeousness.   The ideal of his youthful fancy was no longer there.   And then it was that he looked back again to that little clinging bud that seemed to have sprung to life and yielded its sweetening influence — all for his sake ; and he felt for the first time how it had twined itself about his heart, how wretched he would be without it.   Do you understand this story, Margaret, my love, my love, my love ?

THE END.

www.ingramcontent.com/pod-product-compliance
Lightning Source LLC
Chambersburg PA
CBHW032121080426
42733CB00008B/1014